Seven Deadly Sins

REAL STRUGGLES FROM REAL PEOPLE

BEACON HILL PRESS
OF KANSAS CITY

Seven Deadly Sins
REAL STRUGGLES FROM REAL PEOPLE

Editor
Mike L. Wonch
Director of Editorial
Bonnie Perry
Writer
Don. W. Welch

All scripture quotations, unless otherwise indicated, are taken from the Holy Bible, New International Version®, NIV®. Copyright ©1973, 1978, 1984, 2011 by Biblica, Inc.™ Used by permission of Zondervan. All rights reserved worldwide. www.zondervan.com The "NIV" and "New International Version" are trademarks registered in the United States Patent and Trademark Office by Biblica, Inc.™

From the New Revised Standard Version (nrsv) of the Bible, copyright 1989 by the Division of Christian Education of the National Council of the Churches of Christ in the USA. Used by permission. All rights reserved.

The internet addresses, email addresses, and phone numbers in this book are accurate at the time of publication. They are provided as a resource. Beacon Hill Press does not endorse them or vouch for their content or permanence.

Beacon Hill Press of Kansas City
PO Box 419527
Kansas City, MO 64141
nph.com

ISBN: 978-0-8341-3538-3
Printed in U.S.A.

10 9 8 7 6 5 4 3 2 1

CONTENTS

Not all snakes are poisonous. Some, like the garter snake, are harmless. Many people have seen these types of serpents over the course of their life, and in fact, even feel confident to pick them up. When people encounter this type of snake, they have no need to worry whatsoever. However, snakes like the water moccasin are very poisonous. A bite from this type of venomous reptile requires immediate medical attention. Some snakes are harmless; others are deadly.

Sin, however, is always deadly. That is, there are no harmless sins. Those that give in to the lure of sin will find that it places a tight grip on their lives and causes more pain and destruction than they ever thought possible. Although some may struggle with a certain sin, the good news is that God can and does forgive and enables us through the power of the Holy Spirit to gain victory over those sins. Sin is lethal, but God's redeeming power is greater.

Seven Deadly Sins: Real Struggles from Real People examines seven of the most common sins that people wrestle with and looks at the ways in which we can evade, deal with, and triumph over each one through the power of God working in our lives.

Rev. Donald W. Welch is a California Licensed Marriage and Family Therapist, professor, ordained minister, and President and Founder of the Center for Enriching Relationships (www.EnrichingRelationships.org). He holds degrees: B.A., M.A., M.Div., M.S., Ph.D. (University of Kansas). Dr. Welch is happily married to his wife, Robin, with two adolescent children, Savannah and Daniel.

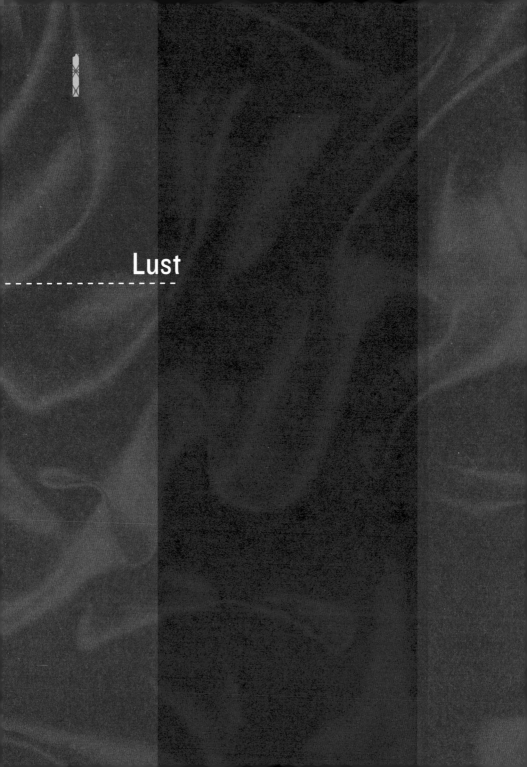

Lust

Elliott and Jessica enter my counseling office. As their therapist I will soon learn that they've been married for a number of years and are at a place they never thought they would be: a pending separation because of Elliot's rampant lust.

Elliott sits down. Without an introduction he immediately shares that his lust if out of control.

Lust. What is it and why is it so powerful and destructive?

Simply put, lust is having an intense desire for someone or something that isn't yours. It is believing you need something, rather than accepting God's embracing love. If not managed biblically, the craving may well consume us. James 1:14-15 describes how we can be tempted, enticed, and then, *"after desire has conceived, it gives birth to sin; and sin, when it is full-grown, gives birth to death"* (v. 15).

We often associate lust with inappropriate sexual wants, but we can lust after so many other things as well: power, control, and food, to name a few.

Whatever the object, lust starts with our thoughts. The apostle Paul instructs the church at Philippi as to what we should yearn for rather than lust after. *"Finally, brothers and sisters, whatever is true, whatever is noble, whatever is right, whatever is pure, whatever is lovely, whatever is admirable—if anything is excellent or praiseworthy—think about such things"* (Philippians 4:8).

Matthew
5:27-30
Phil. 4:8

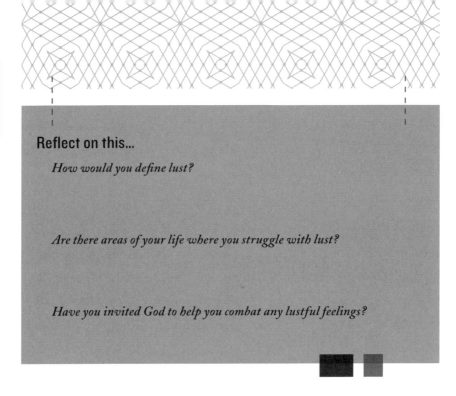

Reflect on this...

How would you define lust?

Are there areas of your life where you struggle with lust?

Have you invited God to help you combat any lustful feelings?

As a church counseling pastor with my own private practice company, I often find myself silently praying for my patients. It's my hope that they will allow God to help them embrace whatever pain they're facing, rather than run from it. These prayers are especially important when the person sitting across from me is battling lust.

In the case of Elliott's private thoughts, lust has ruined his life. It's been said that who you are in public is perception; who you are in your mind and heart is character. Elliott's character is flawed, and needs a heart-felt nature change—not just a behavior change.

Out of all the seven deadly sins, lust wreaks the most carnage of all. Elliott is a prime example.

Paul clearly states in 1 Corinthians 6:18, *"Flee from sexual immorality. All other sins a person commits are outside the body, but whoever sins sexually, sins against their own body."* Although the Bible is crystal clear that all sins receive full forgiveness through Jesus Christ (1 John 1:9), lust leads a person down the most slippery of slopes—often to where a person may well lose everything they've worked for and most treasure. A spouse, children, a home, a job, a reputation.

This idea of taking advantage of a brother or sister—even if just thinking about another person lustfully—is crossing a boundary. Some describe it as defrauding another person. Jerome (writing on Ephesians 5:3) has a phrase which carefully expresses the sense: *"transgredi concessos fines nuptiarum,"* meaning "to transgress the permitted bounds of marriage."

Ephesians 5:3 reads, *"But among you there must not be even a hint of sexual immorality, or of any kind of impurity, or of greed, because these are improper for God's holy people."*

Reflect on this...

In what ways can lust seem so enticing?

Why is there a temptation to want something that's not ours?

What is it within human nature to desire that which isn't ours?

Although sexual lust is seriously harmful, lust for money, power, or control can have devastating results as well. I am reminded of an interview with a billionaire mogul. Apparently, this person likes to have bragging rights in demonstrating who's the wealthiest in his circle. When asked why, he says, flippantly, that it's human nature to want more. To want what you don't yet have.

It's sort of like the cartoon of two cows, each with their individual heads reaching through the other's fence, trying to get the grass from the other cow's field. The caption reads: *Discontented.*

Discontentment without God's presence always leads to destruction. For this billionaire, lust may be attempting to fill a void only God can.

The Bible is clear in that we lust because we are trying to fill the void where only a personal relationship with Jesus satisfies. This billionaire mogul appears to believe he doesn't have enough—he needs more. That's discontentment. That's at the root of lust. Wanting something more, or something that's not yours.

During therapy I often uncover things from a persons poorly developed childhood. I've seen multiple times over these many years of counseling: an unhealthy marriage resulting from childhood wounds and subsequent unhealthy self-medicating behaviors. Unhealthy people depend on self through addictive behaviors of alcohol, drugs, and sex; healthy people ultimately depend on God.

Reflect on this...

If you are struggling with this sin, is something in your past fueling lust?

Is there a professional counselor available to help you?

Would you be willing to talk with your pastor?

Often, lusting turns into addiction. Lustful thoughts are like a careening train with no breaks. We act out, which quickly turns into guilt and shame; the result is compensatory behavior. It goes like this: a person has a lustful thought, hangs onto the thought, it cycles—similar to the hamster running as fast as he can in his cage's spinning wheel without going anywhere except in circles—and then acts on it.

Like a train that barrels off track, wrecking everything in its path, lust, when unattended, destroys everything in its way. For many, it leads to the death of their marriage and the cause of extensive trauma to their children.

It's no wonder God gave us the Ten Commandments. At least three focus on lust in one way or another. For example:

- **The first commandment** (Exodus 20:3) says we must not worship any other than God. We lust after power. We all want more, without God's restraint, our lust is to become a god.

- **The sixth commandment** (Exodus 20:14) tells us to not commit adultery. This rule clearly instructs how not to lust after someone other than your marriage mate.

- **The ninth commandment** (Exodus 20:17) says not to desire your neighbor's wife. Nothing could be more clear as to how to avoid lust.

So, how did can a person get help? And, how can you get help? It is certainly no easy task. For starters, admit the lust. This begins the necessary steps toward healing. Following awareness, confess your sin, becoming determined to turn from your sin. Then, join a serious accountability group where the accountability partners are honest.

Additionally, individual therapy with a Christian professional is needed in some cases, and may or may not be needed in your life.

Although your lust may not have reached the level of Elliott, you may need to seek help. For starters,

- First, ask **God for help.** He wants you to experience a pure life.

- Second, **ask for God's forgiveness.**

- Third, **talk with your pastor** or a trusted accountability partner who understands biblical truths surrounding lust. God knows this is a challenging area of any person's life. God wants to help you live life to the full (John 10:10*b*)!

- Fourth, **develop consistent spiritual disciplines of prayer,** Bible reading, fasting, and church attendance; continually inviting God into all areas of your life.

2

Gluttony

It's a balmy 72-degree day in July. My family and I are attending a professional baseball game, and I'm digging through our bulging backpack full of snacks. In addition to the popcorn and peanuts from home, my lap holds a burger and a hot dog, and I'm juggling a lemonade. Ice cream is next on the menu!

I'm feeling relaxed and carefree, albeit slightly uncomfortable with all the stuff hitting my stomach, and then I notice the guy in the row below us. This is his fourth time out of his seat and back, each time clutching a new foamy brew.

I look at him and think to myself, *Wow, what gluttony.*

Wait a minute. What have I just consumed? If he's guilty of the sin of gluttony, aren't I as well?

Prov 23 : 19 - 21

One definition of gluttony is the act of overconsumption or overindulgence in food. Yet Proverbs 23:21 says *"drunkards and gluttons become poor, and drowsiness clothes them in rags."* Why, then, isn't gluttony considered just dumb and destructive behavior, instead of sin?

1st Corint 6 : 19 - 2

Keep in mind that gluttony is not about your body size. Gluttony becomes a sin when your food consumption is no longer managed by you, the consumer; it's consuming you. As the New Testament communicates, "... *Whose God is their belly"* (Philippians 3:19). Does your belly control you; or do you control your belly? Does eating become an attempt to fill a void that cannot be satisfied by food? Does food distract you from an issue that needs to be addressed in your life?

Gluttony is a combined act of the heart and of the will. Take for instance the person gorging once in a while, or practicing bulimia because of trauma or drinking one's self to death because of self-hatred. Is this sin? Yes, if your behavior is self-medicated driven rather than God driven. It's the comfort of God that satisfies—with the Holy Spirit leading us in healthy living, not human impulse.

As Paul wrote to the church at Corinth: *"Praise be to the God and Father of our Lord Jesus Christ, the Father of compassion and the God of all comfort, who comforts us in all our troubles, so that we can comfort those in any trouble with the comfort we ourselves receive from God"* (2 Corinthians 1:3-4).

Reflect on this...

How would you define gluttony? Do you consider gluttony a sin?

When does over-indulging in food become a sin?

What are the ways we can guard ourselves from living excessively in other areas of our lives?

Let's make another distinction. It was easy for me to justify my overeating at the ballgame and then assume my fellow fan's nonstop drinking was a lifelong problem. Actually, my perception of our drinking friend may have been influenced by my private practice with alcoholics. But putting aside whether I was judgmental or professionally perceptive, this brings up the issue of gluttony being *episodic* or *chronic*. That's psychology jargon for once in a while rather than constant.

How is chronic gluttony different from periodic misbehavior?

Take for instance someone who daily gorges themselves and then as soon as possible purges (vomits) the gluttony away.

Gluttony can be quite complex. Could it be that these individuals' desires cause them to eat and drink out of anxiety? It certainly isn't simply fulfilling nutrition and bodily needs.

For me, occasionally getting away to a ballgame lowers my overall stress. I'm with those I most treasure, and I think my relaxed state tricks me into believing I'm hungrier than essential nutritional needs my body requires. It may be a way of letting me know my overall life is a bit too stressful. Typically, during my everyday life, I don't gorge myself like I do at a baseball or basketball game (unless, of course, my wife stocks the freezer with cookie dough ice cream!).

But for some, clearly their behaviors are chronic and life threatening. Because of that, they fit into "sin" category. If we willfully choose behavior out of the will of God, sin is present. Our bodies are the temple of God, and should be treated as such (2 Corinthians 6:16).

What causes these types of behaviors?

For one person, she began her gluttony behavior at about the same time she discovered something about one of her close family members. She hadn't put together the idea that her eating disorder is related to the pain for this family member until we invited other family members into the therapy room. It was quite surprising for her to realize her eating disorder indicated a need to have some sort of control in her world corresponded to this family member's behavior.

Another example is Billie, whose parents cruelly belittled her. This verbal torture continued to haunt this person. She couldn't find release and permission to honor herself in a healthy way.

You might say she is unable to apply the Great Command of Jesus: *"Love your neighbor as you love yourself"* (Mark 12:31). She couldn't take the risk of loving herself, which rendered her unable to love others.

Reflect on this...

In what ways are issues from your past still affecting you today?

Are you being controlled by excessive behaviors today?

What are the ways you can find help to control these behaviors?

Success in overcoming addictions correlates with the addict's commitment to getting well. Jesus faced this truth on several occasions. In John 5:6, Jesus sees a man who had laid by the pool as an invalid for 38 years and asks him, *"Do you want to get well?"* What an interesting question. Jesus has a way of asking the most healing of questions in perfect timing.

Although we don't know all of this man's plight, we do know that in verse 7 he indirectly expresses a need beyond his physical ailment--friendship. *"I have no one to help me into the pool when the water is stirred. While I am trying to get in, someone else goes down ahead of me."*

We all are made for connection; and, when that doesn't work well, we suffer mentally, emotionally, and spiritually. Jesus obviously understands that, and promises blessings on *"the poor in spirit, for theirs is the kingdom of heaven"* (Matthew 5:3).

I regularly meet with my marriage and family interns. After completing their terminal (a graduate degree allowing them to seek license in the state of California), they are required to be under the supervision of a licensed psychotherapist while they complete 3,000 hours of face-to-face therapy with clients. During these weekly two-hour supervision groups, the concept of a client's desire to get better is a constant discussion.

Typically, this is how it goes. The individual, couple, or family enters therapy eager for change and health. At approximately three sessions into the relationship, the person's pain begins to arise. If the pain is not examined and dealt with, it takes over the sessions until the person who was once eager for healing and health is suddenly done with therapy. They want to stop all onward motion. In other words, the person's pain overrides the person's desire to change.

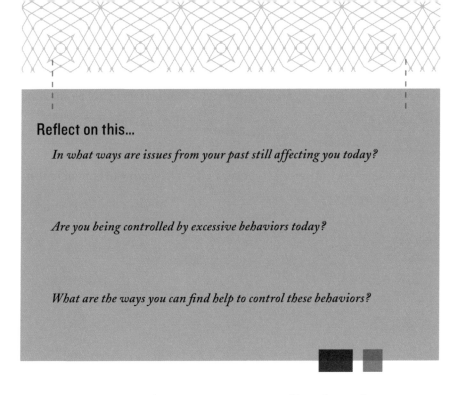

Reflect on this...

In what ways are issues from your past still affecting you today?

Are you being controlled by excessive behaviors today?

What are the ways you can find help to control these behaviors?

What steps can you take in managing or controlling gluttony?

- First, **invite God into this area of your life.** You may be secretly using this controlling portion of your life to meet some unmet need of past or present.

- Second, **meet with your medical doctor for advice.** You may need medical treatment.

- Third, **talk confidentially about it with your pastor or a friend or loved one.**

- Fourth, **find ways in replacing the gluttony behavior with positive behaviors:** healthy breathing, good nutrients, consistent exercise (as recommended by your medical doctor), and most importantly, and enriching relationship with Jesus!

Perhaps you could also consider joining a support group related to your situation. This may include Overeaters Anonymous, Alcoholics Anonymous, Alcoholics Anonymous 12 Step, Al-Anon (for family members of alcoholics), and others.

Gluttony is manageable with God's help. He wants us to allow His comforting presence in every area of our lives. Will you invite Him in to that area of your life?

3

Greed

In the New Testament, why does Jesus spend more time talking about money and greed than He does prayer? Matthew 6:21 speaks clearly to this mystery: *"For where your treasure is, there your heart will be also."* Holding too tightly to something easily leads to the crushing spirit of greed, similar to holding a young bird too tightly crushes its dainty bones.

Greed is excessive or reprehensible acquisitiveness. God speaks against this, and desires better for us. In the New Testament, Jesus spends more time talking about money and greed than He does prayer. In fact, there are 500 verses in the entire Bible about prayer, but there are 2,000 verses about money. Here's one: *"For where your treasure is, there your heart will be also"* (Matthew 6:21).

Here's another, recorded by Luke, a medical doctor, who gets to the heart of things: *"Then he said to them, 'Watch out! Be on your guard against all kinds of greed; life does not consist in an abundance of possessions'"* (Luke 12:15). And Hebrews 13:5 instructs to *"Keep your lives free from the love of money and be content with what you have, because God has said, 'Never will I leave you; never will I forsake you.'"*

Greed sells. Advertising, television shows, and the entertainment industry rake in fortunes while exploiting this human craving. People without God's internal compass are left feeling they never have enough. They always want a little more than they have. Or, as John D. Rockefeller—the oil baron was asked as to how much is enough—responded with: "One more dollar."

How is a Christian supposed to respond to the in-your-face-greed mantra while living in an affluent-laden society?

The Bible explains how it's not how much money you have but how closely you hold it. Mark 12:42-44 helps us with this: *"But a poor widow came and put in two very small copper coins, worth only a few cents. Calling his disciples to him, Jesus said, 'Truly I tell you, this poor widow has put more into the treasury than all the others. They all gave out of their wealth; but she, out of her poverty, put in everything—all she had to live on.'"*

John Wesley put it into a memorable maxim:

"Earn all you can, give all you can, save all you can."

Reflect on this...

In what ways might you be greedy?

Are there times when you desire more than you have? If so, why?

How can you be more aware of this behavior?

During my fourteen years as professor in MidAmerica Nazarene University's religion department, one of my more fulfilling experiences was the yearly mission trip. After half a year of preparation, my wife, Robin, and I would take off to a developing country with 20 or so students.

And, predictably, upon initial interactions with the people of that particular country, the response of our students would be "Wow, these people have nothing, yet they are happy."

This was a true reflective moment for these students—realizing greed doesn't satisfy. The entire trip was worth it all for these young adults to understand that excessive or reprehensible acquisitiveness doesn't fulfill.

I thought back to these students' powerful statements recently when our daughter, Savannah, returned from her Christian high school's Haiti mission trip and said, "Dad, I feel a bit uncomfortable with all that we have."

If you think about it, greed may be considered the opposite of contentment. When contentment seems as far away as your pay increase needed to care for your rent increase, anxiety is present. Say your landlord raises your rent higher than what you can afford. The gap between your paycheck and your rent check might well be an analogy for your lack of contentment!

That anxious feeling tells you that something's not quite right.

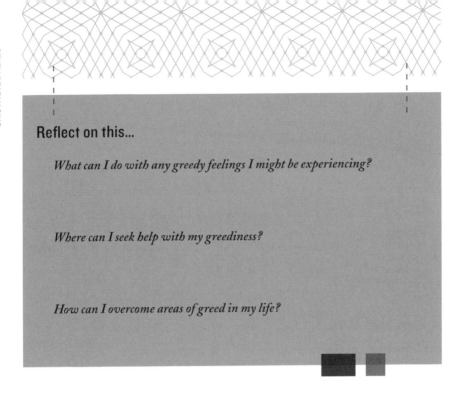

Reflect on this...

What can I do with any greedy feelings I might be experiencing?

Where can I seek help with my greediness?

How can I overcome areas of greed in my life?

Even though my university students are the most amazing human beings, I'm frequently surprised with how easily they get jittery and outright anxious without their personal cell phones, Facebook, Twitter, and all of the comforts of their laptop computers. They appear to want more and more media. I hear comments like this:

"Can I get one more *like* on this photo?"

"I found this awesome jacket at my favorite clothing store."

"Did you see the latest fashion on this website?"

"I have 513 friends on Facebook."

In Philippians 4:11, Paul instructs about contentment when he says, *"I am not saying this because I am in need, for I have learned to be content whatever the circumstances."*

Mr. Carson is tall, handsome, and dressed to impress in his custom-made suit. Mr. Carson started off pursuing a major he felt God leading him toward. However, perceived poverty of this career led Mr. Carson to abandon his call in exchange for the prestige and financial rewards of stock trading.

Only at the point of his wife leaving him and his losing much of the wealth he had worked so hard to accumulate did Mr. Carson begin the painful process of evaluating his life. He lives with a deep sense of regret.

Ecclesiastes 5:10 says, *"Whoever loves money never has enough; whoever loves wealth is never satisfied with their income. This too is meaningless."*

I wish I could say Mr. Carson is an isolated incident. Unfortunately, it's not. It's epidemic.

I've sat with many people in similar cycles of pain and regret, especially since the Great Recession. I remember hearing repeat stories of other people like Mr. Carson. The financial downturn had hit, and the emotional destruction caused by greed was wiping people out like a tsunami.

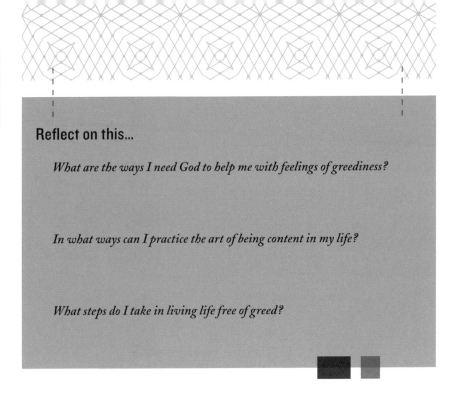

Reflect on this...

What are the ways I need God to help me with feelings of greediness?

In what ways can I practice the art of being content in my life?

What steps do I take in living life free of greed?

What's enough for you? What can we do with this sin of greed?

First, we must turn to God asking Him to help us take captive our thoughts. 2 Corinthians 10:5 says, *"We demolish arguments and every pretension that sets itself up against the knowledge of God, and we take captive every thought to make it obedient to Christ."*

Are you training your mind toward the things of God, or are you ruminating on the things of this world? It's a simple equation. You need most, if not all, of your thoughts aimed at God's economy rather than your greed.

Second, spend daily time asking God His purpose for you. He'll inform you; you'll experience more contentment; He's interested in doing so. You will enjoy His compassion and contentment.

NOTES:

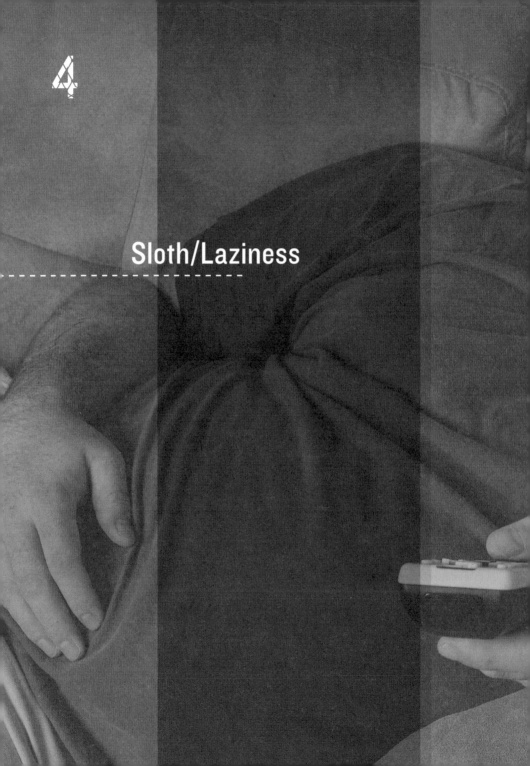

4

Sloth/Laziness

Prov 15:19

I'm good at avoiding certain things. Take for instance, staying on a consistent exercise routine.

Prov. 24: 30-34

Given enough time and space, I find almost any excuse for avoiding this discipline. Yes, I always feel better once the pain of exercise subsides and I'm benefitting from natural runner's high. Yet, staying with a daily routine, with its demands of discipline beyond the lazy streak within me, I easily default to my nature of lazy and even slothful behaviors. Do you suffer from this also?

Laziness means being disinclined to activity or exertion: not energetic or vigorous. Sloth is an inability to take initiative. Proverbs 15:19 says, *"The way of the sluggard is blocked with thorns, but the path of the upright is a highway."* Do you find yourself lazy or even slothful? When you can't seem to find the necessary energy to accomplish the task at hand?

Even though you're initially determined to push through and wanting to complete the task, you lack the discipline or ability for follow through. This is the problem. You've heard the ole adages:

"Inch by inch, it's a synch." "No pain no gain." "Just fight through the pain."

That's all good and well; yet, when it comes to consistent and repetitive follow through, and where your running shoes meet the road, people can be lazy and slothful.

Eph 4: 26-27 29-32

Take for instance my counseling patients. Initially, the patient is quite enthused about possible results. Once you tap into the pain, the client recoils much like a turtle does when poked or prodded. There can be an instant recoiling into its shell. I frequently experience my patients responding in a similar way: enthusiasm for anticipated healing overridden by pain.

Although initially it appears to be laziness/slothfulness, emotional pain overwhelms. And, the patient will do almost anything other than embrace it.

Those of us in the mental health field call these behaviors emotional defenses. This is when someone defends their behavior while at the same time blaming someone else or some object for it. You've experienced this. You try and give corrective encouragement to someone you care about only to be met by them finding some fault in you as a distraction from the topic at hand. This behavior is better known as "displacement."

You may have seen this in a relationship of yours. It's similar behavior to the person—after coming home from a bad day at work—trying to get rid of frustrations while yelling at the family dog, or worse, family members. The proverbial verbiage describes the dog as having done nothing wrong; nonetheless, the master kicks or berates his dog.

It's a common experience—a way of trying to detox emotions by displacing it onto someone or something else. Unless you're skilled in the area of awareness, you also do this. (Not necessarily kicking your dog; but acting out on someone or something!)

You may try to convince yourself you don't displace. However, it's a defenseless debate. Denial is in and of itself displacement. We all displace our emotions, unless of course we've become aware that we are doing it which helps us in better controlling the behavior. It's at the heart of lazy/slothful behavior.

Take a moment and reflect on how you may take out your anger by displacing it onto—say your family or coworkers. Romans 7:15 clearly speaks of and describes what happens when we live without awareness. The apostle Paul clearly states that if we are under the law without God's Holy Spirit's awareness, you will say to yourself: *"I do not understand what I do. For what I want to do I do not do, but what I hate I do."* This behavior is displacing your feelings and responsibility onto to someone else or some object.

Reflect on this...

Why do some people become lazy in certain areas of their lives?

What are actions people do based on their lazy/slothful behavior?

How can we become more aware of our behavior?

Without discipline in finding ways not to blame others, we will do the very thing we are trying so hard not to do. Bottom line, you may attempt to make yourself feel better without taking full responsibility for the emotion and situation.

It's very similar to Adam's behaviors toward Eve in the Garden of Eden. Following their disobedient eating from the tree of knowledge of good and evil and hiding from God and each other (remember how they covered their nakedness once they ate from the tree?), God's asked them in Genesis 3:11, *"Who told you that you were naked? Have you eaten from the tree that I commanded you not to eat from?"* Then in verse 12, *"The man said, 'The woman you put here with me—she gave me some fruit from the tree, and I ate it.'"*

Adam's displacement (an act of deflecting) of the question can be seen in many if not all areas of a person's life. We don't like God, or anyone else, questioning us. You may often find yourself distracting a conversation to something other than the topic in discussion. That's when you displace it onto someone else or some object; you deflect (displace) your feelings while blaming someone else. Does this sound familiar?

For eight years straight, my wife, Robin, and I have taught a year-round couples' class at a large church in San Diego County. With 60 to 75 couples per week, we frequently notice this lazy/slothful theme. A wife will come up to me and say, "He won't do the class assigned homework." A husband says to me, "I'm tired of her haranguing me about everything she thinks I should be doing." These are typical exchanges. Neither spouse is able to see his or her behaviors, similar to Adam and Eve's. It's much easier blaming someone else than taking full responsibility.

Let's take a closer look at what's behind our displacing or blaming others—a lazy or even slothful way of behaving. Jake and Laura show signs of slothful behavior. Laura is demanding and a bit stubborn, while Jake does what he wants when he wants. Both lack discipline—especially in the area of healthy interactions with each other.

The couple has adequate financial wealth, allowing neither having to spend much time working for income outside of the home. Their financial security—coupled with their lazy and undisciplined communication challenges combine in producing slothful behavior.

Jake says he wants a better relationship with Laura; however, he can't pull himself away from the sports channel. According to Laura, he watches 24/7. Laura claims that Jake does nothing around the house other than watch sports. He says he is tired of Laura's constant badgering.

Although this emotional exchange may seem simple and direct, it isn't. Their language is actually distracting at something other than the real issue. They are displacing their individual frustrations on to the other. Neither is taking responsibility for their actions and behaviors. They have yet to download basic communication 101, where one speaks and the other validates and offers respect and empathy.

Jake wants attention and respect. Rather than ask for it directly, he continues ignoring Laura and she displaces her anger through belittling him; although they may have a form of zeal and affection for the other. This is a common cycle for unhealthy couples. Jake and Laura need an infusion of discipline and zeal for one another, rather than being so lazy and slothful. The New Testament instructs in Romans 12:11, "Never be lacking in zeal, but keep your spiritual fervor, serving the Lord."

Reflect on this...

Why do couples behave as Jake and Laura?

What are ways Jake and Laura can discipline their behaviors?

How can this couple better manage positive interactions with each other?

What do I say to the patient who displaces like Jake and Laura? Initially, the person needs to admit he or she behaves this way. Quite often, if you can't admit to a certain behavior, it's because of fear.

In the Garden of Eden, Adam was afraid of how God would view him and respond to him had he told God the truth upfront. With our mates, friends or loved ones, we're afraid of how they might view us; or worse, give up on us and abandon us. These fears cause us to avoid the real issues, leading oftentimes to displacement.

Second, we must figure out the feeling/experience behind the awareness. Are you feeling afraid, insecure, embarrassed? Name those.

Finally, own them. Many people are insecure in their own abilities, which leads to a lack of owning their own experience. It's this lazy—perhaps even slothful—way of tackling an issue that gets you into the most trouble. It leads us into many different forms of slothful behaviors.

Practice the following:

- Admitting

- Awareness

- Ownership

Tonya shows signs of this slothful behavior. Her appearance is disheveled and quite anxious. She is in her early 40s, wants marriage, but continues in an emotional pattern of overeating, under sleeping, overcommitted and taking very little pride in her health. Tonya's behaviors could be labeled lazy and slothful. Yet, the underlying issue is fear.

For some, laziness is a result of fear--preventing us from what we desire. Isaiah 41:10 speaks to this debilitating fear, *"So do not fear, for I am with you; do not be dismayed, for I am your God. I will strengthen you and help you; I will uphold you with my righteous right hand."*

For those who experience fear leading to lazy and slothful behaviors, each needs to:

- **Admit the fear.** Which can be the most difficult and challenging step. Although naming and claiming the fear can be like wrapping your arms around a porcupine. It hurts to do so. Yet without doing so, you'll remain a turtle locked up in its hardened shell.

- **Awareness leads to embracing the pain.** The more one is emotionally aware of what they're experiencing (emotional intelligence) the better one is to managing pain rather than it controlling the person.

- **Ownership.** This means not avoiding the reality of the pain; rather, one is doing what is necessary to take responsibility of the pain.

5

Wrath/Anger

I was on the freeway heading to my university classes after a stressful visit to the hospital. A guy whizzed pass me and flipped me off. Not only that, his face was full of wrath and I had no problem reading his lips.

"Get off the road, you idiot!" he yelled. "You're driving too slow! You're going to kill someone!"

Anger is powered by indignation or frustration; wrath is anger-motivated desire for punishment. This strong emotion is part of the famous "fight or flight syndrome." An angry person is poised ready to fight an attacker, or to flee the situation. Or, possibly, the angry person is frozen—in a helpless sort of position. These reactions, built into us by God, are His way of helping us survive danger. They also can work against us.

Think about a car screaming down the freeway in first gear. The engine is about to explode. That's like a person's emotional system when angry. Without proper management, an angry person is stuck in first (emotional) gear, revving up emotion to explosive levels.

The question is, why is anger listed as one of the seven deadly sins? Is anger always a sin? When is it not? After all, the Bible says God gets angry, and Jesus was angry enough with the money changers in the temple that He drove them out and overturned their tables. And how do we learn to how to be angry and not sin (Ephesians 4:26)?

Not all anger is sin. The difference has to do with what's at the core of anger and what you do with the anger--your behavior.

Look at Ephesians 4:26. The apostle Paul instructs, *"In your anger do not sin: Do not let the sun go down while you are still angry."*

Ephesians 4: 26-32

Mike and Deb have a 16-year-old son, Kent, who recently was suspended from school for alcohol use. Mike is angry and often shouts at Kent because of his behavior. Deb doesn't say much. Kent feels the real problem is his dad. Kent and his parents is a classic case of anger and sin. Mike was psychologically and verbally abusing Deb. Kent was full of anxiety and anger, and sought relief through alcohol use. All the while, Mike was taking no responsibility for his abusive behaviors.

While this family's out-of-control situation may seem extreme, there are elements in it that we all must face.

Jesus illustrated righteous anger while clearing the temple. He set a boundary while defining the temple as a place of worship and not a market place. His anger helped him not back down. The opposite of Jesus' controlled anger is out-of-control anger, with no regard for others.

The Bible clearly describes the difference between controlled and out of control anger. Genesis 4:6-8 says, *"Then the lord said to Cain, 'Why are you angry? Why is your face downcast? If you do what is right, will you not be accepted? But if you do not do what is right, sin is crouching at your door; it desires to have you, but you must rule over it.' Now Cain said to his brother Abel, 'Let's go out to the field.' While they were in the field, Cain attacked his brother Abel and killed him."*

Cain experienced anger. God confronted him. Cain then was faced with choosing between right and sin. He chose sin over good, ending up killing his brother.

Typically, an angry person has a hard time admitting wrathful behavior. Cain is one example.

Mike was no different. He was defensive and didn't believe he was being mean. His sinful anger had roots to his own father. It was difficult for Ben separating painful childhood wounding from his impulsive anger toward his wife and son. His wife and son were the victims of his sinful anger.

Through counseling, prayer, and the support of others, Mike became aware of his sinful anger and began to understand his motivations and patterns of behavior. Mike moved from sinful anger to righteous anger and an increased relationship with Jesus—and his family.

In dealing with wrath and anger, Proverbs 15:1 instructs: *"A gentle answer turns away wrath, but a harsh word stirs up anger."*

This passage makes so much sense when we understand how God created our emotions. During moments of anger, we can't simply stop our feelings. It's not as simple as snapping your fingers and instantly softening intense feelings. We must first calm down. And, this can take a few minutes; and, sometimes up to an hour or two.

Proverbs warns against harsh words and stirring up anger. While in the midst of anger, remember: the best antidote is empathetic (active) listening rather than convincing the other person they're in the wrong.

When feeling angry, you're actually anxious. Anger and anxiety always co-exist. The guy on the freeway cussing me appeared angry. Yet, underneath all of his verbosity was actually anxiety and fear. He really needed someone to tell him it is going to be okay. Obviously, I wasn't the person who could help; I was the problem.

What do you do when you are angry? First, find ways to better calm yourself. This could be reading the Psalms, singing a chorus or hymn, or even taking a deep breath of fresh air while exhaling twice as long as inhaling. All of these can bring calm and peace. Each of us needs nurture when we're angry.

A child with a skinned knee needs compassion and care much more than the obvious small bandage. Likewise, in your anxious moments, you need someone to help your mind and body work together. God's active and living Word helps us in Philippians 4:6-7, *"Do not be anxious about anything, but in every situation, by prayer and petition, with thanksgiving, present your requests to God. And the peace of God, which transcends all understanding, will guard your hearts and your minds in Christ Jesus."*

Reflect on this...

Why do some people have problems with anger?

What are ways have more self-control with anger?

How can we better manage anger with each other?

Children are naturally impulsive. They want what they want; and they want when they want it. As the parent shapes the child's impulsive behavior, the child grows up learning how better to respond than reacting to life's turns and tunnels. Resisting the urge to lashing out at others is important to emotional and spiritual health. The art of self-control assists the child, and then adult, to managing his/her emotions rather than spontaneously giving into the emotion at any given moment.

Learning this self-control skill is similar to delay of gratification. It is one of life's more important skills. It's what most parents are trying to teach when saying something like this:

"No snacks between now and dinner—you'll just have to wait until dinner time."

The parent is teaching the child the art of self-control. It's learning that soothing hunger pains is not as important as managing the impulse. We encourage this same skill to the one needing anger management; self-control while not giving into the impulse.

If an impulsive child does not learn this skill, given enough time and repeated angry situations, he or she becomes an impulsive adult lacking self-control. This, then, leads to fighting as a way of life: getting what he/she wants and when he/she wants it.

Earlier, we talked about the fight anger impulse. The second anger defense—better known as "flight—typically causes the person to running away when angered. Several of my patients call their mates a "runner." Meaning he or she runs every time there is conflict.

Many people do this without knowing what they're doing. In marriage, we call this person the *distancer*. The *pursuer* is the one wanting to solve an issue at that moment; whereas the *distancer* is the one who may need more time to think it through; or, simply compelled to run from the problem.

Also, you have the person who freezes when there are disagreements. They have no idea what to do with the anger. So, they do nothing; freeze.

Anger is like stepping too close to a cliff. There's a point of no return. Getting too close may plunge you to your death. So is anger. Left unmanaged, you get closer and closer to the edge of the anger cliff, until without awareness, you explode and plunge to your emotional death. This emotional explosion seriously damages you and sends shrapnel into others.

Many of my angry male clients describe this experience as recognizing some frustration (like getting closer to the cliff's edge), and they then black out without awareness (like plunging off the cliff). The rage goes viral, similar to the latest breaking news on social media. It's out of control. They are completely unaware of falling off the emotional cliff. The only awareness is when they are pulling their hand out of the dry wall.

God wants better for us. He wants us managing our anger with godly behaviors. Here are steps toward managing your anger:

- Develop an awareness of when your body tightens in frustration.

- Relax those tension-filled areas of your body.

- Name the anxious feeling: "I'm afraid," "I'm frustrated," "I'm sad."

- Embrace those feelings until you're keenly aware of them.

- Grieve those negative feelings by praying, crying, or speaking them in confidence to another person.

- Remember to breathe.

NOTES:

6

Envy

Have you ever gone to work only to discover your colleague has received the promotion you thought was yours? Or, perhaps your neighbor is moving to a part of town you've only dreamed of living in. Or, your friend's daughter has received a full scholarship to a great university while your son barely squeaks by with a "C" average in high school.

If you've struggled in situations like these, then you know envy. Envy is a painful or resentful awareness of an advantage enjoyed by another, joined with a desire to possess the same advantage. In other words, envy is craving what you don't have. Whereas, jealousy is worried someone's attempting to take what is yours.

Envy may be one of the most underestimated sins, but it's one that the Bible confronts head-on. 1 Peter 2:1-2 says, *"Therefore, rid yourselves of all malice and all deceit, hypocrisy, envy, and slander of every kind. Like newborn babies, crave pure spiritual milk, so that by it you may grow up in your salvation."*

Speaking of babies, early on my wife and I observed our two toddler children envying each other's toys, friends, attributes—you name it, they envied it. Envy appears to be part of fallen human nature. Unless dealt with early in life, a child grows up envying what their neighbor has: the newest car, the latest cell phone, that spectacular home, those extravagant vacations.

All of us have a bit of aggrandizement/narcissistic tendencies. We may even believe we deserve what someone has worked hard for. It's likely you don't fit the full criteria for narcissistic personality disorder. Believe me, if you had this disorder, you would be miserable, your family and friends would be frustrated with you, and you would have a diminishing social life. Or, at the least, you might be wondering where your friends went, since people want to get away from a narcissist.

According to the *DSM-5 Diagnostic and Statistical Manual of Disorder*, "Individuals with narcissistic personality disorder are often preoccupied with fantasies of unlimited success, power, brilliance, beauty, or ideal love."[1] The manual further states "These individuals are often envious of others or believe that others are envious of them."[2]

Here's a disturbing thought: Although only a small percentage of the population is diagnosable as narcissistic personality disorder, there is research suggesting that this personality disorder is becoming more common.

Certainly, without spiritual and mental awareness, narcissistic symptoms can creep into anyone's life. Take for example the phrase, "I want what they have." It can apply to a number of desires, from toys to possessions and prestige and job status.

God is concerned about how we think about and view ourselves and others. Romans 12:3 tells us, *"...Do not think of yourself more highly than you ought, but rather think of yourself with sober judgment, in accordance with the faith God has distributed to each of you."*

Tom and Addie are an example of the dangers of envy. Addie wasn't dealing well with the necessary sale of their expensive home and cars. She blamed her husband and thought he was the cause of all their problems. Further sessions revealed more about Addie, and changed the focus of the therapy. It became obvious that Addie was consumed with envy. She was upset and angry at other people's wealth and prestige.

This couple was caught in a viscous circle, she would spend more which would cause Tom to work more. It was emotional tug-and-pull. Addie's envy

1. *Diagnostic and Statistical Manual of Mental Disorders*, 5th Edition, (American Psychiatric Publishing, Washington, DC, 2013), 670.

2. Ibid, 671.

needs were never satisfied and Tom worked more hours hoping to earn more income. Addie spent more money, hoping to satisfy her yearnings. Yet, no one was satisfied.

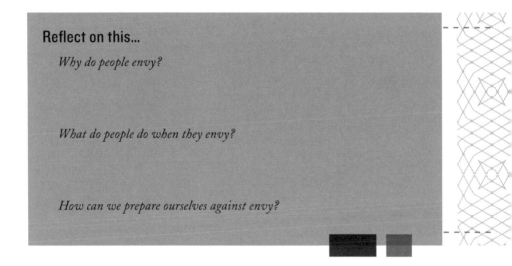

Reflect on this...

Why do people envy?

What do people do when they envy?

How can we prepare ourselves against envy?

If you're struggling with envy, first ask yourself where the desire is coming from. Is it from childhood? Does it have roots in an adult experience? Is it tied to something more recent? If nameable, how can you grieve the memories/experiences so you can let go of the pain?

Quite often, persons envying others have difficulty appreciating what they have. They're never satisfied. Life is just not quite good enough. This lack of self-appreciation often translates into unable to appreciate others. These are the two narcissistic symptoms: grandiosity and lack of empathy. The key to healing is identifying and grieving the feelings behind these experiences.

For Addie, she never feels good enough. Do you feel this way?

Envy has a way of reaching deep within a person while tugging at the very core of self-worth. Do you suppose that might be one reason why Jesus spent most of His earthly mission validating people and relationships?

Matthew 20:13-15 addresses Addie's issue while describing an owner hiring people during one day's work hours while at the end of the day giving each a denarius pay regardless of when they were hired. The workers who had been there all day grumbled unfairness, to which the owner replied: *"...Didn't you agree to work for a denarius? Take your pay and go. I want to give the one who was hired last the same as I gave you. Don't I have the right to do what I want with my own money? Or are you envious because I am generous?"*

Reflect on this...

Why do you envy?

What behaviors do you display because of your envy?

How can you grieve this envy?

All family mental health literature says for children to be emotionally and physically healthy, they need to know they are deeply loved. And parents who have been deeply loved know best how to deeply love their children. That's why Christians who are deeply in love with Jesus experience His unmeasurable love—and can raise the healthiest children on this planet.

It's a biblical truth: If you know you're loved, you love in return (and vice versa). 1 John 4:7-8 expands on the idea. *"Dear friends, let us love one another, for love comes from God. Everyone who loves has been born of God and knows God. Whoever does not love does not know God, because God is love."*

What do you envy? Is it something you didn't get in the past? Or, is it something you must grieve and let go.

I can't help but think of Jesus' enormous grief over loss. He lost His family, His reputation, His character (because being without sin He took on the sin of the world), yet He never envied. Why is that? Well, we know He was fully God and fully man. Yet in His full manhood, He continually went to the Father for His self-love and His love for humankind. Rather than focusing on what He didn't have in this world (envy), He focused on what He is in God. Jesus was God's beloved Son in whom I am well pleased.

How can you focus on the Lord and what you have through Him rather than envying?

- Daily thank God for your health.

- As you are getting up in the morning, thank the Lord for something you're anticipating.

- Have, "An attitude of gratitude."

- Simply smile at your loved ones.

- And, smile at yourself in the mirror.

- Sing a favorite hymn or chorus.

NOTES:

7

Pride

I remember my dad's retirement party. Friends and family came from around the country to celebrate his milestone with him. Dad's accomplishments as a college professor were outstanding. I was bursting with pride.

Before the event, I decided to prepare a videotape to share of all of his awards and publications, including five published university math textbooks. I started taping the family home, zooming in on family photos, souvenirs, Dad's books, and his favorite chair. Then I realized something was missing. Where were Dad's doctorate and master degrees? As I realized that Dad never put his degrees in frames on the wall, I remembered a comment made by my father's best friend, Jim. They had been buddies since childhood.

While my father was completing his Idaho State University doctorate in mathematics, his best friend said to him, "Lee, when you get that degree, you'll be too smart to be my friend."

I've never asked Dad about his friend's statement, but from the day he received his doctorate, he has discouraged anyone from calling him "Dr. Welch." In fact, I've never seen him sign his name using "Dr.," or use it on envelopes or on documents. I guess when it comes to pride, Dad has always taken Proverbs 16:18 seriously.

What is sinful pride? What is healthy pride? How can you tell the difference, and how do we foster the good kind and protect against the bad kind?

First, it's important that we understand healthy pride and healthy self-esteem. When your child shows you his latest and greatest drawing, he's working on his self-esteem. That's healthy pride. A child believes in herself to the degree to which you believe in her. "Wow, honey, that's spectacular," is something a healthy parent might say. We're attempting to build into the child healthy pride and healthy self-esteem. You've heard people say their greatest gift in life was that someone believed in them. God set it up this way. A child knows he/she is valued by a caregiver letting him/her know so.

As adults, we know we're of value because God's values us. This important concept helps us understand how healthy or unhealthy pride can be. Take for instance Philippians 2:5 speaking of Jesus:

> In your relationships with one another, have the same mindset as Christ Jesus: Who, being in very nature God, did not consider equality with God something to be used to his own advantage; rather, he made himself nothing by taking the very nature of a servant, being made in human likeness. And being found in appearance as a man, he humbled himself by becoming obedient to death—even death on a cross.

Jesus, fully God and fully man, maintained an unawareness of His power as God. He humbled himself to the place of servanthood. Void of any pride, Jesus demonstrated His heart being in the right place: fully focused on God. His life is God's way of demonstrating ultimate pride-less-ness.

I often ask my university students, "How do you know if you're humble?" In other words, how do you know if you're without sinful pride? Think about that for a moment. Can we really know if we are humble? Can a human be accurately aware of his or her own humility? Without God's quiet voice (the Holy Spirit) speaking into our lives, probably not. On the other hand, we can realize when we are prideful. One way of analyzing this is that if you think you are humble, you're not. Once you believe in your humbleness, you're now prideful.

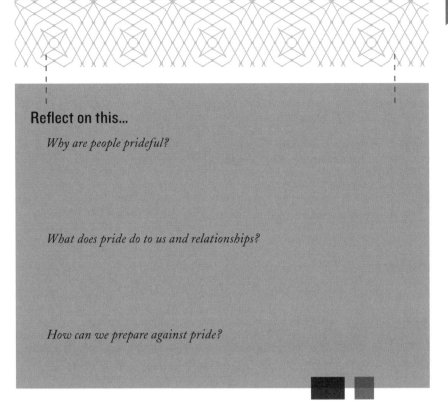

Reflect on this...

Why are people prideful?

What does pride do to us and relationships?

How can we prepare against pride?

Jesus' relationship with the Father demonstrates humility. He wanted only to do the Father's will. Throughout the New Testament we see Jesus putting His relationship with the Father before everything and anyone. When needing time alone with the Father, He delayed His ministry (Luke 6:12). While praying to the Father, Jesus committed to honoring the Father above all ("Glorify your Son, that your Son may glorify you." John 17:1). When seeking the disciples' humility, He prayed to the Father, *"that all of them may be one, Father, just as you are in me and I am in you. May they also be in us so that the world may believe that you have sent me"* (John 17:21).

So humility is the opposite of sinful pride. Yet, we need to be careful. If we view any type of pride as sin, we may likely go the other extreme—defining healthy self-esteem as sin also. It's like saying because eating food can cause cancer, I choose not to eat any food. That's a bit foolish. We know that some foods have cancerous effects; yet, deciding not to partake of any nutrients will certainly end in death.

We need a bit of healthy pride for nurturing self-esteem. And, self-worth and self-esteem are an integral part of a health personality.

Children help us in understanding the importance for healthy pride and self-esteem. Last evening, while my daughter, Savannah, was completing homework assignments, we started talking about her homecoming, graduation, and university prospects. She asked if I wanted to see her high school final transcript. I was delighted while reading and discussing it with her.

After reading her transcript summarizing her past four years, I looked up and said,

"Wow, honey, you must be very proud of yourself. This is an amazing transcript! Your mom and I are very proud of you! You couldn't have done any better than you have. You gave it your best efforts, and the results show it. Congratulations Annie-Doll (my nick name for Savannah)!"

Savannah's eyes lit up while bursting with pride. I went on to say,

"You are an amazing person."

Full of healthy pride and strong self-esteem, my daughter is headed into an adult life. She's an example of pride without sin. There's a difference between healthy pride and self-esteem and sinful pride.

Jesus summarizes healthy pride and self-esteem, *"...I have come that they may have life, and have it to the full."* And, He pointed us to the Father and not His accomplishments in John 14:6, *"...I am the way and the truth and the life. No one comes to the Father except through me."* Jesus' commitment and continual focus was in the right place: on God.

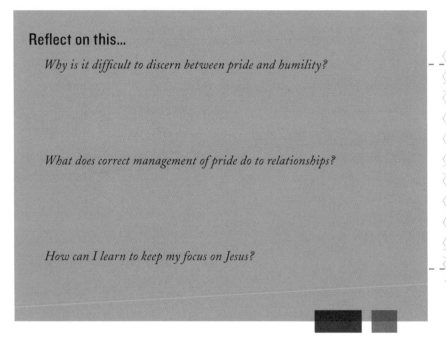

Reflect on this...

Why is it difficult to discern between pride and humility?

What does correct management of pride do to relationships?

How can I learn to keep my focus on Jesus?

How do we live out humility rather than pride? Jesus makes it clear in Matthew 28:18-20, *"All authority in heaven and on earth has been given to me. Therefore go and make disciples of all nations, baptizing them in the name of the Father and of the Son and of the Holy Spirit, and teaching them to obey everything I have commanded you. And surely I am with you always, to the very end of the age."* All of our work, relationships, and efforts are for the purpose of modeling, and pointing people to Jesus. That's it; nothing more, nothing less.

Regardless of your vocation, you have responsibility to God to live out this mandate in pointing people to Jesus! Everything else pales in comparison. It is the humility of Christ.

Is your focus on this world, or Jesus and eternity? If it's on this world, you're leaning into pride. If it is Jesus, your humility will grow. Where's your focus?

The following steps will help you manage pride and sin:

- **Take inventory of what is more important to you than your relationship with Jesus.** If you spend more time with it than you do with God's interests, it is pride.

- **Ask God to show you things, persons, status, etc. that keep you prideful in who you are.**

- **Invite the Holy Spirit in showing you whose you are in Christ rather than who you are in and of yourself.**

- **Daily allow the Holy Spirit to keep your conscience about pride in check.** 1 Timothy 1:18-19 says, *"Timothy, my son, I am giving you this command in keeping with the prophecies once made about you, so that by recalling them you may fight the battle well, holding on to faith and a good conscience, which some have rejected and so have suffered shipwreck with regard to the faith."* The Holy Spirit will prompt your conscience in knowing the difference between pride and healthy self-esteem and humility.

- **In your small group, ask a friend to share his or her view of your humility and pride.**

- Be open to your family's view of your pride and humility.

- Daily pray and ask God if there's any sinful pride in you.

NOTES: